DIGGING UP DINOSAUR FOSSILS IN

EUROPE

DIGGING UP DINOSAUR FOSSILS

Little Mitchie
an imprint of Mitchell Lane

Creating Young Nonfiction Readers

Little Mitchie lets children delve into nonfiction at beginning reading levels. Young readers are introduced to new concepts, facts, ideas, and vocabulary.

Tips for Reading Nonfiction with Young Readers

Talk about Nonfiction

Begin by explaining that nonfiction books give us information that is true. The book will be organized around a specific topic or idea, and we may learn new facts through reading.

Look at the Parts

Most nonfiction books have helpful features. Our *Little Mitchie* titles include color photographs and graphic aids, a table of contents, a glossary, and an index. Share the purpose of these features with your reader.

Color Photos and Graphic Aids

A lot of information can be found by "reading" photos, charts, maps, and other graphic aids found within nonfiction texts. Help your reader learn more about the different ways information can be displayed.

Table of Contents

Located at the front of the book, this list shows the big ideas within the text and the page numbers where they can be found.

Glossary

Located at the back of the book, the glossary defines key words and phrases that are related to the topic. These words and phrases can be found in the text in colored type.

Index

Located at the back of the book, an index is an alphabetical list of topics and the page numbers where they can be found.

With a little help and guidance about reading nonfiction, you can feel good about introducing a young reader to the world of *Little Mitchie* nonfiction books.

Mitchell Lane
PUBLISHERS

2001 SW 31st Avenue
Hallandale, FL 33009
www.mitchelllanepub.com

Little Mitchie

First Edition, 2025.

Author: Meg Greve
Designer: Rhea Magaro
Editor: Madison Greve

Names/credits:
Title: Digging Up Dinosaur Fossils in Europe / by Meg Greve
Description: Hallandale, FL : Mitchell Lane Publishers, [2025]

Series: Digging Up Dinosaur Fossils
Library bound ISBN: 979-8-89260-241-9
Paperback ISBN: 979-8-89260-418-5
eBook ISBN: 979-8-89260-246-4

Little Mitchie is an imprint of Mitchell Lane Publishers.

PHOTO CREDITS
Alamy: Stocktrek Images, Inc., 12-13; Shuttertock: Michael Rosskothen, cover, 1, 8-9; Colorcocktail, cover, 1 (sign); Elenarts, 3; Aust28, 4, 6, 9, 11, 13, 15, 17, 18, 20, 23; Noiel, 5; WavyBxl, 6-7; Dotted Yeti, 10-11; rodos studio FERHAT CINAR, 14-15; Catmando, 16-17; Daniel Eskridge, 18-19; Gorodenkoff, 20-21

CONTENTS

When Dinosaurs Ruled the Land

Sea levels are high. A group of islands disappear and reappear over time. Dinosaurs must live, eat, fight, and roam across the hot and steamy land. This is Europe before it was a **continent**. This was the time of the dinosaurs!

Before there were seven continents, all land formed one giant continent called Pangea.

Paleontologists are scientists that study dinosaurs. They have discovered many **fossils** all over Europe. These fossils tell the story of our planet, more than 200 million years ago.

DINO DETAILS:
Dinosaurs that hunted on land used sharp claws and even sharper teeth to catch smaller animals.

Meat for Dinner? Meet the Carnivores!

Megalosaurus was a large **carnivore** who walked on two legs. It hunted **prey** in forests. It had a huge head with a mouth full of sharp teeth.

DINO DETAILS:
Some dinosaurs have been discovered with the bones of other animals inside of their stomachs! This tells us what they liked to eat.

Compsognathus was small, but very fast. It had hollow bones that made it easy for them to run after smaller prey. Some paleontologists believe it could have had feathers.

DINO DETAILS:
Although dinosaurs lived millions of years ago, many of them look like animals that exist today.

Baryonyx had more than 90 teeth! It used its strong jaw and claws to catch slippery prey, like fish. It also had a long skull that looked like a crocodile's.

DINO DETAILS:

Herbivores only ate plants. But those with long necks could do two things at once to keep themselves safe.

More Plants for the Herbivores, Please!

Plateosaurus was a common herbivore. It ate plants and looked out for **predators**. Its long neck helped it see enemies from far away and reach the tops of tall trees.

DINO DETAILS:
The Hypsilophodon had a small beak that helped it eat and tear leaves from trees.

Hypsilophodon fossils were found grouped together. This tells paleontologists that these dinosaurs lived in groups. They were able to run at high speeds. Its tail was held straight out for balance.

Iguanodon was about 30 feet (9 meters) in length. It had teeth that could chew and grind the plants it grabbed with its front feet. It also had spiked thumbs.

DINO DETAILS:
When paleontologists first found the thumb spike they thought it was a horn, like a rhinoceros has.

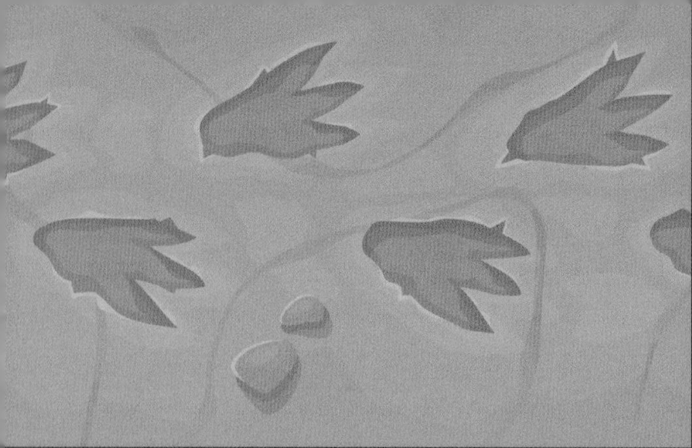

Dinosaurs may have lived millions of years ago, but they may still seem alive to us now. New fossils are found every day. They tell the story of the time when dinosaurs ruled Earth.

Where Did the Dinosaurs Live?

More than 300 different dinosaur fossils have been found in Europe. These are just a few!

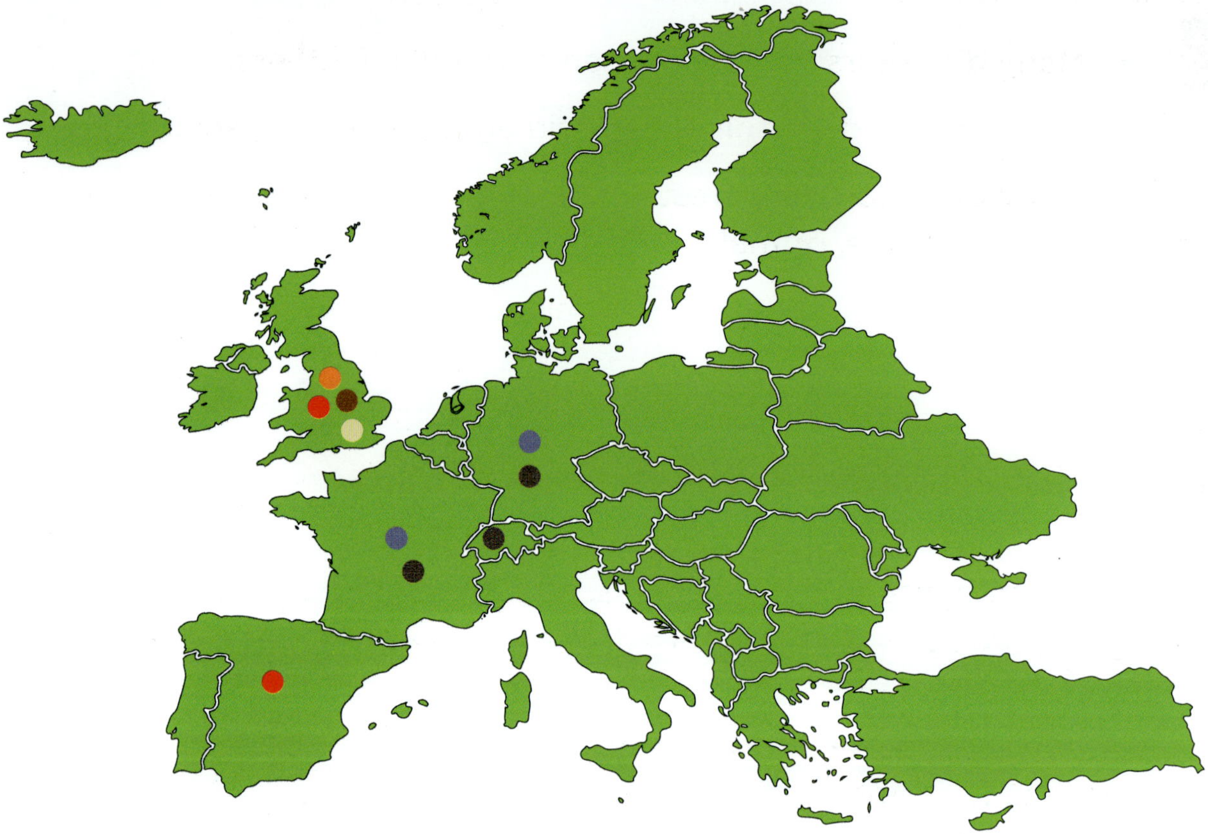

- **Megalosaurus:** England
- **Compsognathus:** France and Germany
- **Baryonyx:** southeast England
- **Plateosaurus:** France, Germany, Switzerland
- **Hypsilophodon:** England and Spain
- **Iguanodon:** England

Interesting Facts

- The word dinosaur means “terrible lizard.”
- Many dinosaurs may have been covered in feathers.
- Larger herbivorous dinosaurs laid eggs as big as a soccer ball.
- Many dinosaurs had crests, frills, and horns used for defense, finding a mate, or making noises.
- Dinosaurs used their tails for balance, defense, and to show off!

Spotlight On: Mary Anning

When Mary was just 12 years old, she found a complete skeleton of an ichthyosaur! She learned about fossils from her father by going on digs with him. Mary did not have the chance to attend school. She taught herself all she could about the earth and sky from reading books and talking to her father. She changed the way many scientists thought about dinosaurs. Sadly, she did not always get the credit she deserved. No matter what other scientists thought about Mary’s accomplishments, history will remember her as an important paleontologist who used what she had to teach the world about dinosaurs.

Glossary

carnivore (KAR-ni-vor):
A meat-eating animal

continent (KON-tin-ent):
One of the seven largest pieces of land on Earth

fossils (FAH-suhls):
Rock that forms after a living thing is preserved in the earth

herbivore (ER-buh-vor):
A plant-eating animal

predator (PRE-duh-ter):
An animal that hunts other animals for food

prey (pray):
Animals hunted and eaten by other animals

Index

Further Reading

Blackford, Cheryl. Fossil Hunter: How Mary Anning Changed the Science of Prehistoric Life. New York, NY: Clarion Books, 2024.

Hansen, Grace. Dinosaur Graveyards in Europe. Minneapolis, MN: Abdo Kids, 2021.

Rubin, Sean. The Iguanodon's Horn: How Artists and Scientists Put a Dinosaur Back Together Again and Again and Again. New York, NY: Clarion Books, 2024.

On the Internet

STEM Career Inspiration for Kids: Paleontologists
https://blocksrock.com/news-and-learning/stem-career-inspiration-for-kids-paleontologists
Learn how to be a paleontologist.

Learn how to be a paleontologist.
List of European dinosaur facts for kids.
https://kids.kiddle.co/List_of_European_dinosaurs
View facts and pictures of dinosaur fossils found in Europe.